God's
Little book of

Calm

Words of peace and refreshment

RICHARD DALY

WILLIAM
COLLINS

William Collins
An Imprint of HarperCollins*Publishers*
1 London Bridge Street,
London, SE1 9GF

www.williamcollinsbooks.com

5 7 9 10 8 6

First published in Great Britain in
1999 by HarperCollins*Publishers*
This edition 2013

A catalogue record for this book is
available from the British Library

ISBN 978-0-00-752832-5

Printed and bound in China by
RR Donnelley APS Ltd.

Introduction

I've written this book to lead you to the true source of all calm. That source is found in none other than Jesus Christ. It is through him that you can ultimately obtain peace in a peaceless world.

Throughout this little book you will find priceless gems of spiritual advice and comfort to help you face the challenges of each day. It is God's will that none of his children become perplexed with the cares and toils of life, for he is more than willing to cover you with his calming presence.

Open this book at any page and claim those precious promises that will bring ultimate peace and calm to your life.

Richard Daly

Know God, know calm ...
no God, no calm

The secret of being calm is knowing the God of calm. The more you get to know him, the calmer and more at peace you will become within yourself.

For Further Reflection

Psalm 46:10

Let God be God

Anxiety is calm's greatest destroyer ... when we are agitated or frightened by events in our lives, let us learn to let God be God and accept his direction and leading.

For Further Reflection

Proverbs 16:3
Philippians 4:6

Seek wisdom

There is security and rest in the wisdom
of the eternal Scriptures.

For Further Reflection

James 1:5

Let God shape you

If you're going through an unusual amount of grief and pain, don't despair. The master potter is at work in your life. He sometimes has to break us so he can remake us.

For Further Reflection

Jeremiah 18:4

Think happiness

Happiness is a product of the mind, of attitude and thought. It comes from you, not to you. To be happy you must choose to be happy: the Scriptures say, 'as a man thinks in his heart, so is he.'

For Further Reflection

Proverbs 23:7

Interrupt yourself

Sometimes a short break can actually help you get the job done faster. When stress threatens your concentration, take a deep breath, relax your muscles and picture yourself in a calm environment. After you've unwound go back to the job.

For Further Reflection

Genesis 2:1–2

Evaluate your day

It may encourage you to ask yourself,
'What was the best thing that happened
to me today?' at the end of each day.

For Further Reflection

Psalm 42:8

Better to give than to receive

The most important thing about giving
is that it imparts values of generosity and
thoughtfulness. Priceless treasures are usually
the best gifts, giving the greatest delight.

For Further Reflection

Acts 20:35
James 1:17

Exercise

If you don't use it, you lose it. That's certainly true of muscle strength. Walking, jogging, cycling or swimming gets the muscles working, the heart beating faster, and the blood whizzing through the arteries. There's the added bonus of a feeling of well-being, produced by endorphins released from the brain during exercise.

For Further Reflection

3 John 2

Choose to relax

Behaviour modification can help you to live a healthier life. In tense situations tell yourself, 'I can't handle everything, but I am in charge of my attitude, and I choose to relax.'

For Further Reflection

Psalm 42:5

Take joy in simplicity

The nicest and sweetest days are not
necessarily those in which anything very
spectacular or wonderfully exciting happens,
but those that bring simple pleasures,
such as the sun sinking like a gold coin
into the pocket of night.

For Further Reflection

Psalm 96:11–12

Know your limits

Those who are happily successful in life are
willing to work hard but know their limits.
For such people work is not everything: they
know how to relax, prize close friends and
spend quality time with their families.

For Further Reflection

Proverbs 4:10–13

Be inspired by water

There's something about water that has an
instinctive, calming influence ... a trickling
river, a crystal fountain, the vast open sea,
a gushing waterfall or a tranquil lake –
such wonders of nature ought to inspire
you with calm and awe.

For Further Reflection

Psalm 137:1

Listen to your body

God in his ingenious, creative design for humankind, has built within us natural alarm signals – headaches, exhaustion, migraine, stress, agitation – to warn us when the pendulum of calm has swung too far. Do yourself a favour and listen to your body.

For Further Reflection

Psalm 32:8

Wrap yourself in God's love

Take God's comfort blanket of unfailing,
unlimited and unconditional love. Then
wrap it snugly around yourself and enjoy
the warmth and protection it offers.

For Further Reflection

Romans 8:35

Stay in touch

During times of void stay in touch with
God: he will fill the holes of our emptiness
with his calming presence.

For Further Reflection

Jeremiah 33:3
Isaiah 26:3

Walk by faith

Each day begin your walk in the calm
trust that God is at work in everything.

For Further Reflection

Lamentations 3:23
Proverbs 3:5–6

Meditate

Most of the time our minds are like water
whipped into waves by the distraction and
pressures of life. We spend much of our
lives in touch only with the choppy surface.
Meditation enables us to calm down, so
the water becomes clear and still.

For Further Reflection
Psalm 104:34
Psalm 19:14

Take shelter with God

In the stormy periods of life God promises,
'When you pass through the waters I will
be with you; and through the rivers they
shall not overflow you.' With him you
can weather any storm.

For Further Reflection
Isaiah 43:2

Someone's thinking about you

God thinks about us all the time; he says,
'I know the thoughts I have toward you ...
thoughts of peace and not of evil, thoughts
to give you hope and a future.'

For Further Reflection

Jeremiah 29:11

Bask in the countryside

Picturesque landscapes – the rolling meadow,
the open fields, the green hills – all add to
the preservation of tranquillity. That's where
God leads ... 'He makes me lie down in green
pastures, he leads me beside still waters,
he restores my soul.' How calming!

For Further Reflection

Psalm 23:1–3

Don't worry!

You can't control the past, but you can ruin a perfectly good present by worrying about the future.

For Further Reflection

Philippians 4:6–7

Ratio 1:100

For every one thing that goes wrong
in our lives, we have more than a
hundred blessings.

For Further Reflection

Psalm 107:38
Psalm 146:5–6

Take God's peace

No human wisdom can explain God's
calming peace. It is a 'peace which passes
all knowledge and understanding'; it cannot
be fathomed, or scientifically explained,
but it will 'guard your heart and mind'.

For Further Reflection

Philippians 4:7

Look to the light

It never hurts your eyesight to look on the bright side of life!

For Further Reflection

Micah 7:7
Titus 2:13

Seek the God of peace

True peace comes first by knowing the God of peace and then by being at peace with him.

For Further Reflection

Romans 5:1

Take God's strength

Whatever the circumstance, whatever the
price, whatever the sacrifice, his strength
will be your strength in your time of need.

For Further Reflection

Psalm 32:7
Jeremiah 16:19

Keep praying

A lot of kneeling keeps one in
good standing.

For Further Reflection

Colossians 4:2
James 5:15–16

Count your blessings

Although pain is inevitable, misery is optional. We can either count calamities or we can count blessings.

For Further Reflection

Malachi 3:10

Reach out

Use what you have to enrich the lives of others and you will soon find your own cup running over with joy.

For Further Reflection
Luke 6:38

Cast your burdens

When you cast your burdens on the Lord,
he will not only sustain you but will replace
them with the sweet experience of calm.

For Further Reflection
Psalm 55:22
Matthew 11:28–30

Be still

He who calmed the troubled sea is
more than able to say to your storm,
'Peace, be still.' What assurance!

For Further Reflection

Mark 4:39
Psalm 107:29

Let Jesus in

When Jesus comes into your life he
brings the calmness of heaven.

For Further Reflection

Matthew 11:28
Psalm 29:11

Pray sincerely

To every sincere prayer he answers,
'Here I am.' What an awesome God!

For Further Reflection
Isaiah 58:9
Psalm 145:18–19

Choose the forever friend

We are never alone, whether we choose
him or not: in Jesus we have a
forever-faithful friend.

For Further Reflection

Proverbs 18:24

Psalm 119:90

Be safe in his presence

One of the characteristics of God is his
omnipresence ... the ability to be everywhere
at any time. Be assured, then, that though
circumstances may separate us from our
friends, no circumstance or distance can
separate us from the heavenly comforter.

For Further Reflection
Psalm 139:7–10

Believe and receive

Rest in the fact that God's compassion and love never change. Jesus said, 'Whatever you ask for in prayer believe that you have received it and it will be yours.'

For Further Reflection

Mark 11:24

Appreciate each new day

Every day is a gift from God; there are so many potential joys that lie ahead. The Psalmist says, 'This is the day that the Lord has made, let us rejoice and be glad in it!'

For Further Reflection

Psalm 118:24

Get ready!

If you have been under attack lately,
get ready; God is about to show you
what the fight was all about.

For Further Reflection

Psalm 27:14

Go to church!

A survey conducted over a period of
28 years concluded that people who attend
church enjoy better health, have lower
blood pressure, less depression and
stronger immunity to disease! Going
to church can't be that bad.

For Further Reflection
1 Chronicles 16:25–29
Psalm 122:1

Avoid emotional burnout

It is not work that wears people out,
but sadness, anxiety and worry. To God all
your griefs are worthy of consideration.

For Further Reflection

Philippians 4:6–7
1 Peter 5:7

Put God first

The secret of fruitfulness is giving God the first part of every day, the first consideration in every decision and the first place in your life. Try it and see what happens.

Do unto others

Once in a while we all need to hear
somebody say, 'I think you're wonderful.'
Encourage someone with these words today.

For Further Reflection

Romans 12:10
Ephesians 4:32

Keep focused

If you want to be miserable, focus on what
others have and forget what God's given you.
Contentment is not getting what you want;
it is enjoying what you've got.

For Further Reflection

Hebrews 13:5
1 Timothy 6:8

Be humble

Learning to be humble will turn things around in your life when nothing else works. Consider these words: 'Humble yourself in the sight of the Lord and he will lift you up.'

For Further Reflection

James 4:10

Avoid needless pain

'Oh, what peace we often forfeit,
oh, what needless pain we bear,
all because we do not carry everything
to God in prayer.'

Joseph Scriven

For Further Reflection

Philippians 4:6
Jeremiah 29:12

Praise him!

To praise is an exhilarating experience.
Go ahead; get over your inhibition,
open your heart, lift up your hands and
begin to praise him.

For Further Reflection

Habakkuk 3:18
Psalm 51:8

Shalom

Jewish people greet one another with the
word '*shalom*'. It means 'peace', 'well-being'
and 'wholeness'. Your heavenly Father is
actually called *Jehovah-Shalom*, 'The Lord
is my peace.' The assurance is that
God lives up to his name.

For Further Reflection
Genesis 22:14
Isaiah 9:6

Live God's today

We spend so much of our lives worrying about yesterday and tomorrow, yet one's buried and the other's unborn. Both are beyond our control ... but remember God is 'a very present help'.

For Further Reflection

Psalm 46:1

Walk by faith

When in faith we take hold of his strength
he will change, wonderfully change, the
most hopeless, discouraging outlook.

For Further Reflection

Psalm 37:39–40

Psalm 62:8

He who numbers the hair on your head

Tell it as it is – he is not indifferent to your needs. Take everything to him that perplexes your mind – nothing is too great for him to deal with.

For Further Reflection

Matthew 10:29–32

Go to the great physician

There's not a sorrow, nor a grievance, nor a human weakness for which God has not provided a remedy. Our heavenly Father has a thousand unknown ways to provide for us.

For Further Reflection

Jeremiah 33:3
Isaiah 65:24
Genesis 18:14

Trust and obey

Our task is not to decipher exactly how all of life's pieces fit together and what they mean, but to remain faithful and obedient to the God who knows all mysteries.

For Further Reflection

Ephesians 1:9
Mark 4:11

Leave it to God

Are you dealing with a difficult situation today? Ask God for guidance ... then leave the outcome to him.

For Further Reflection

Proverbs 4:11–12
John 16:13

Seek roses amongst thorns

We all need to become like avid rose
gardeners, hunting for buds of beauty
within our thorny circumstances.
It's a sure cure for complaining.

For Further Reflection

Genesis 1:31
Psalm 90:17

Accept God's sacrifice

The joyful message of the gospel is that
God through Jesus' sacrifice on Calvary
has made it possible for our sins to be
completely forgiven.

For Further Reflection

John 3:16
Isaiah 1:18

Just trust him

If in our difficulties we trust in the Lord
as our strength, he will do even more than
give emotional relief: he will enable
us to rejoice.

For Further Reflection

1 Corinthians 10:13

Think what God thinks

When we have done our best to serve
the Lord, a thoughtless or critical remark
can take away our joy. When that happens
you must focus instead on what God
thinks about you.

For Further Reflection

1 Samuel 16:7

Affirm

Words of affirmation will always create
an atmosphere in your home that's
conducive to calm and repose.

For Further Reflection

Titus 3:8

Be positive

It takes less energy to say something positive than it does to say something negative. In fact, doctors now say that when we speak positive words our bodies relax and the blood flow actually increases to our brain – and a well-oxygenated brain will always help us to handle situations more effectively.

For Further Reflection

Colossians 4:6

Deposit love

Relationships are like bank accounts:
they're either in deficit, or in balance, or
in surplus. No deposit ... no return!

For Further Reflection
1 John 4:7, 11
Jude 25

Fear not

The words 'fear not' are used 365 times
in the Bible. That means there's a 'fear not'
for every day of the year.

For Further Reflection

Isaiah 41:10
2 Timothy 1:7

Your guardian angel

Did you know you have a guardian angel
keeping protective watch over you each
day and night? The Scriptures say, 'He shall
give his angels charge over you, to keep
you in all your ways.'

For Further Reflection

Psalm 91:11

Take God's insurance policy

You have a divine insurance policy that guarantees complete coverage against fire, flood, and death. He promises that even though you walk through the valley of the shadow of death you will fear no evil, for he is with you.

For Further Reflection

Psalm 23:4

Be touched by the
master designer

Psychiatrists say our behaviour is
determined by our parents and by our
environment. But when Jesus becomes the
Lord of your life, neither nature nor nurture
can prevent you from becoming the object
of beauty he intends you to be.

For Further Reflection

Jeremiah 18:4–6

Seek God's wisdom

We can say with confidence that while God's purposes and plans are very different from ours he is infinitely wiser than we are and his timing is always perfect.

For Further Reflection

2 Samuel 7:28–29

Let God solve it

God knows you better than you know
yourself, and he can do for you that which
you can't do for yourself.

For Further Reflection

Psalm 139:4
John 21:17

You're not alone

You're not alone today. He promised to be
with you through the darkest night. He'll
rock you to sleep in the bosom of his love
and cradle you in the palm of his hand. Even
when others turn their backs on you,
he will never leave you nor forsake you.
Aren't you glad you have him?

For Further Reflection

Psalm 50:15

Genesis 28:15

Don't be afraid

If you're afraid of the future, just check
the past. Has he ever failed you? No ...
and he never will.

For Further Reflection

Joshua 21:45
Joshua 1:5

Wait on the Lord

A stress-filled mind always makes it harder
to hear what God's saying to you. So just
wait in his presence. When the time's right
he'll give you clear direction.

For Further Reflection

Psalm 27:14

Isaiah 40:31

Change your attitude

Our greatest discovery is that we can alter
our lives by altering our attitudes ... it's your
thought life, not your circumstances, that
determines your happiness.

For Further Reflection

Philippians 2:5

Don't quit

We're all fighting a battle of some kind,
but some are not winning! Winners have
one thing in common: a strong faith
that refuses to quit.

For Further Reflection
1 Timothy 6:12
Joshua 23:10

Climb higher

Be like the hawk: when it's attacked by crows it doesn't counter-attack. That would be unproductive! No, it simply soars higher and higher, until the pests leave it alone. Lighten your challenges by soaring higher on wings of faith.

For Further Reflection
Isaiah 40:31

Seize the moment

Today there are opportunities all around
you to make a difference in the lives of
others ... seize them!

For Further Reflection
1 Thessalonians 5:11

Look out!

Whatever you're facing today, never
for one minute think that you can't cope.
When you've run out of strength and can't
fight on, God will send reinforcements ...
so start looking for them!

For Further Reflection
Psalm 16:8

Have faith

Faith is a walk in the dark with your hand
firmly planted in the hand of God whom you
cannot see. It is determining to trust God
even though he has not answered all your
questions. Such faith will inevitably lead
to peace of mind.

For Further Reflection

2 Corinthians 5:7

Encourage one another

If you meet somebody today who
needs encouragement, go ahead and give
it to them – more people die of broken
hearts than swelled heads.

For Further Reflection

Hebrews 10:25
1 Thessalonians 5:11

Claim God's love

Many descriptions of God given to us in
Scripture depict him as infinitely loving
and kind. His love 'always hopes, always
perseveres ... it never fails.'

For Further Reflection
1 Corinthians 13:7–8

You'll never walk alone

If you're struggling on your own to face
the challenges, then you need to know
you're not alone! 'The God of all comfort
is with you.'

For Further Reflection

2 Corinthians 1:3

Appreciate small things

It's the little things which reveal the chapters
of the heart – the little attentions, small
incidences and simple acts of kindness that
make up the sum of life's happiness.

For Further Reflection
Luke 16:10

Your unseen helper

Who knows how many times the Lord
quietly protects us, redirects us or leads
us on safer paths?

For Further Reflection

Psalm 23:3

Keep the commandments

The Ten Commandments still have their place. The first four enhance our relationship with God, while the last six helps us to love other people. Obeying God's law leads to ultimate calm.

For Further Reflection

Matthew 22:37–40
Exodus 20:3–17

Use your secret weapon

Secret prayer is your powerful tool against
life's conflicts – it provides you with divine
rays of light to strengthen and sustain you
in the dark hours of life.

For Further Reflection

1 John 5:14
Matthew 21:22

Step out in faith

The best thing about the future is that it is
offered to you a day at a time ... though you
may not know what the future holds you can
calmly say, 'I know who holds the future.'

For Further Reflection

Revelation 1:8
James 4:14–15

Quiet things

Just quiet things – a serene stream, sweet-
scented dusk, the gentle rain, the hush before
the morning bird first sings – can all fill the
soul with deep contentment and peace.

For Further Reflection
Isaiah 32:18

Smile!

Whereas depressive moods can
negatively affect the flow of blood
in the brain, smiling people produces
anti-stress hormones which are an
ingredient of calm.

For Further Reflection

Proverbs 17:22

Take a walk

Physical activity, which helps to relax
the muscles and generate a healthy 'glow',
can be achieved simply by a brisk
15-minute lunchtime walk.

For Further Reflection

3 John 2

Enjoy the fragrance of flowers

So sensitive are the human nervous system, mood and temperament that flowers may stimulate metabolic changes. They bring refreshment and raise the spirits. Enjoy their fragrance and calming beauty.

For Further Reflection

Songs 4:13–14

Sleep well

The way we handle our emotions has a lot to do with how well we sleep. An internal clock known as the circadian rhythm controls the process of assimilation and body metabolism. Sleep is important for good health and a calm nature.

For Further Reflection

Proverbs 3:24
Ecclesiastes 5:12

Avoid noisy places

Eighty decibels (from a loud radio or snoring) can induce pain, is hazardous to heart patients and can cause stress. There is such a thing as constructive silence: it conserves vital energy.

For Further Reflection

Ecclesiastes 3:7

Breathe fresh air

Fresh air provides you with 60 per cent of your energy. Breathe a few deep breaths ... then slowly exhale all your worries away.

For Further Reflection

Jeremiah 30:17
3 John 2

Accept Christ's rest

Rest is the essence of calm. That's why
Jesus said, 'Come unto me and I will give
you rest.' Being with Jesus ultimately
leads to calm.

For Further Reflection

Matthew 11:28
Psalm 37:7

Promises, promises!

The Scriptures contain over 3000
promises of help – more than enough
to meet every human need.

For Further Reflection

2 Corinthians 1:20
Joshua 23:14

Don't relive past mistakes

Do not be perturbed about past mistakes and sins. Jesus, your ever-forgiving friend, promises that he will separate them from you as far as the east is from the west.

When you remind God of some past sin he responds, 'What sin?'

For Further Reflection
Psalm 103:12

Look ahead

We may see much that discourages us.
The forces of evil seem to be in control.
But if by faith we look beyond the present
and focus on the wonderful home God
has prepared for us, we will find much
reason to rejoice.

***

For Further Reflection
2 Peter 3:13

A mighty God

Though he holds up the world and
rules over the affairs of the universe ...
nothing that troubles our peace is too
small for him to notice.

For Further Reflection

Psalm 59:16
Isaiah 54:10

He's alive

Our greatest comfort in life is to
know that Jesus is alive!

For Further Reflection

Mark 16:6

Be of good cheer

The shortest verse in the Bible, 'Jesus wept,'
provides us with the greatest insight: we have
a friend who has experienced all the griefs
and pain that we experience today.

For Further Reflection

John 11:35
Mark 1:41

Let bygones be bygones

To hold a grudge is like sprinkling salt on an
open wound. Let bygones be bygones and
experience the healing effect of calm.

For Further Reflection

Luke 11:4

Luke 6:37

Slow down

Don't get caught up in the so-called rat-race of life. Next time you go out, purposely slow down or stop if you need to: let the handiwork of nature declare to you the glory of God.

For Further Reflection

Psalm 19:1

Be Christ-centred

Don't allow circumstances in life to control you: be Christ-centred, so that he can control the circumstances in your life.

For Further Reflection

Isaiah 42:16
Nahum 1:7

Avoid late nights

'Early to bed, early to rise' is an old-fashioned formula for stress-free living. Try relinquishing this routine: you may find that the principle behind it still works.

For Further Reflection

Mark 1:35
Proverbs 6:10

Seek reconciliation

Letting the sun go down on your wrath is a
precursor for insomnia; the better option is
to endeavour to seek reconciliation. With that
purpose in mind you will already experience
the engulfing effect of calm.

For Further Reflection

Ephesians 4:26
2 Corinthians 5:18

Let God take control

He who numbers the very hairs on your
head does not fail to notice your moment
of need. To him all your disappointments
are his appointments.

For Further Reflection

Matthew 10:30
Deuteronomy 31:8

Think highly of yourself

In God's estimate you are the 'apple of his eye': his thoughts toward you are as though you are the only person living in the world. What an awesome God!

For Further Reflection

Zechariah 2:8

Claim the riches

As a child of God, you are an heir to his kingdom. That means you also share in his inheritance ... which means that whatever belongs to God belongs to you! He promises, 'I will supply all your needs according to my riches in heaven.'

For Further Reflection

Galatians 4:7
Hebrews 9:15
Philippians 4:19

Don't forget God's blessings

Take comfort. We have nothing to fear
for the future, unless we forget the way
the Lord has led us in the past.

For Further Reflection

Proverbs 16:3

Take sides with God

Few things are more intimidating than our fears and our worries, especially when we face them in our own strength. Be assured of this promise: 'If God is for us who can be against us?'

For Further Reflection

Romans 8:31

Accept the challenge

God is never at a loss to know what he's going to do in any given situation. He knows perfectly well what is best for us – our challenge is simply to trust him.

For Further Reflection

Proverbs 3:5–6
Psalm 62:8

Let God handle it

When you face an impossibility, leave it in
the hands of the specialist. He won't
necessarily handle it your way, but he'll
handle it. 'The things that are impossible
to us are possible with God.'

For Further Reflection

Luke 1:37
Luke 18:27

Pass the buck

When you see the beginning of anxiety ...
at that precise moment pass it on to
the Lord.

For Further Reflection

Psalm 55:22

Untie the knots

Worry drains our energy and makes us
tired. Untie those knots of anxiety with
the settled assurance that the Holy Spirit
is your comforter and guide.

For Further Reflection
John 14:26

Don't get strangled

Our English word 'worry', is from the
Dutch *worgen*, which means 'to strangle'.
Worry, if allowed to persist, will strangle
us to death!

For Further Reflection

Philippians 4:6–7
Matthew 6:25–31

Be patient

Those who wait on the Lord will gain
new strength. But remember: the key
to the Lord's strength is waiting.

For Further Reflection

Isaiah 40:29–31

Listen

The best part of praying is being still
long enough to listen.

For Further Reflection

Psalm 17:6
2 Samuel 22:7

Let your weakness be your strength

The weaker and more helpless you know yourself to be, the stronger you will become in his strength. The heavier your burdens the greater the joy in casting them upon the great burden bearer.

For Further Reflection

2 Corinthians 12:9–10

Seek refuge in God

The Lord would like everyone to come to
him as their refuge for counsel and for
comfort. To him you may tell all your griefs;
you will never be told, 'I cannot help you.'

For Further Reflection

Isaiah 41:13

Hebrews 13:6

Let God be God

God has numerous ways to provide for
his children. He says, 'Call unto me and
I will show you great and mighty things,
which you know not.'

For Further Reflection
Jeremiah 33:3

Rejoice always

Developing a consistent attitude of praise
and adoration triggers a feeling of wellbeing.
Take God's advice: 'Rejoice in the Lord
always and again I say rejoice.'

For Further Reflection
Philippians 4:4

Seek peace

True peace is that inner contentment
that pervades even in times of adversity.
Jesus says, 'My peace I give unto you.'

For Further Reflection
John 14:27

Be still

When all else fails on a stressful day, just
'Be still and know that I am God.'

Laugh away

Laughter is release and the best pick-me-up available; so let laughter have its way. Remember, 'A merry heart does good like medicine.'

For Further Reflection

Proverbs 15:13
Ecclesiastes 3:4

Remember the Sabbath

Knowing that work and the stress of life can cause fatigue, God has given us a special day of rest. It's called the Sabbath ... one day in seven God tells us to take time out for him!

For Further Reflection

Exodus 20:8

Meditate on good things

'...whatever is true, whatever is
noble, whatever is right, whatever is
lovely, whatever is honourable ...
meditate on these things.'

For Further Reflection

Philippians 4:8

Read a psalm

The book of Psalms contains the most wonderful words of comfort and reassurance. Read a portion from time to time – you're sure to find something that will encourage you.

For Further Reflection

Colossians 3:16

Trade places

If you know a real test is coming, talk to the Lord about it; then trade with him. Hand over your fragility and receive his strength and wisdom.

For Further Reflection

James 1:5
2 Thessalonians 3:3

Share the problem

If 'a problem shared is a problem halved',
then tell it to Jesus twice.

For Further Reflection

Psalm 17:6
Isaiah 59:1

Fix the jigsaw

Jesus is the central piece of life's puzzle.
If we fit him into place the rest of the puzzle,
no matter how complex and enigmatic,
will begin to make sense.

For Further Reflection
1 John 5:12
Colossians 3:4

Accept yourself

Calm comes with accepting yourself for who you are. When God develops your character, he works on it throughout a lifetime.

For Further Reflection
Philippians 1:6

Have Jesus as your mentor

Life is a schoolroom. In it we encounter
quizzes and periodic examinations. You
can't have a course without tests,
but if Jesus is your mentor he will
provide all your answers.

For Further Reflection

Genesis 18:14
Jude 25

See failure as success

It is easy to get discouraged over failure.
Instead of seeing apparent failures as
obstacles, see them as stepping-stones
to success.

For Further Reflection

Job 22:28
1 Peter 1:13

Give God the glory

Our major goal in life is not just to be
happy or satisfied, but to glorify God.
If we do this we will be more than
happy and satisfied.

For Further Reflection

Psalm 146:5
Psalm 20:5

Be comforted

It's always comforting to know
that someone is there in times of
deepest need.

For Further Reflection

Hebrews 13:5–6

Let God fix it

God does not offer temporary relief;
he offers a permanent solution.

For Further Reflection

Isaiah 54:10
Haggai 2:4–5

Take one day at a time

God gives us just enough light to see
the next step, and that's all we need.

For Further Reflection

Psalm 27:1

Psalm 23:2

Invest with God

Entrust. What a wonderful word! It is a
banking term meaning 'to deposit'. When it
comes to trials, we deposit ourselves
into God's safekeeping and that deposit
yields eternal dividends.

For Further Reflection

Ruth 2:12

Recharge each day

The Lord's unfailing love and mercy
will always continue fresh as the morning,
as sure as the sunrise.

For Further Reflection
Lamentations 3:22–23

Give love away

There's a chorus that says, 'Love is something if you give it away; it comes right back to you.' Try it and see if it works.

For Further Reflection
1 John 4:11

Whatever you wish

Treasure this Bible promise: 'Delight
yourself in the Lord and he will give you
the desires of your heart.'

For Further Reflection

Psalm 37:4

Keep a record

Count your blessings one by one.
Write them down; keep a record.
You will be amazed to discover what
the Lord has done.

For Further Reflection

Deuteronomy 28:2
2 Corinthians 9:8

Respond calmly

Quarrelling can be a major source of
stress. Follow the advice of Solomon,
'A harsh word stirs up anger, but a soft
answer turns away wrath.'

For Further Reflection

Proverbs 15:1

Begin with prayer

Begin the day with prayer. Your mind
will be refreshed and you will be braced
to face the day's challenges.

For Further Reflection

Isaiah 55:6

Claim this promise

'Be strong and of good courage; do not
fear nor be in dread of others, for the Lord
your God who goes with you, he will
not fail you nor forsake you.'

For Further Reflection
Deuteronomy 31:6

Share your smallest problem

We sometimes fail to bring our problems
to God because they seem so small ... but if
they're large enough to vex us and endanger
our welfare, they are large enough to
touch his heart of love.

For Further Reflection

Psalm 42:5

Hold on

In those moments of deepest
despair, take courage ... 'weeping
may endure for the night but joy will
come in the morning'.

For Further Reflection

Psalm 30:5

Imitate Christ

If we substitute peace for calm, the following
text reads, 'my calm I leave with you, my calm
I give you'. It's this calm and unruffled spirit,
which was so obvious within Christ's life,
that we too can have today.

For Further Reflection

John 14:27

Believe God's word

'For no matter how many promises God
has made, they are "Yes" in Christ.'

For Further Reflection

2 Corinthians 1:20

Find quiet time

It's good to have a daily 'quiet time',
an opportunity every day to give God
time to speak to our lives as we
meditate on his word.

For Further Reflection

Psalm 19:14

Psalm 46:10

Relax

God is 'the God of all comfort, who
comforts us in all our tribulations'.

For Further Reflection
2 Corinthians 1:5–4

See yourself as God sees you

It's easy to look at ourselves and feel
worthless and hopeless. The good news
is that your value is established by God's
estimate, not yours! Get your opinion
of yourself in line with God's!

For Further Reflection

Psalm 40:5
Psalm 139:17

Enhance your self-esteem

Don't say, 'I'm not good enough.' If that's
true, then you're God's first mistake, and God
doesn't make mistakes. He doesn't love you
because you're valuable – you're valuable,
because he loves you! Let that sink in.

For Further Reflection
John 3:16

Think big

Next time somebody asks you, 'Who do you think you are?', lift your head, square your shoulders, and confidently reply, 'I am a child of God; I'm bought with a price; I'm loved with an everlasting love; I'm blessed coming in and going out; I'm the head not the tail ... and if you have a few more hours to spare, I'll tell you the rest!'

For Further Reflection
Jeremiah 31:3
1 Peter 2:9

Live in grace

Grace is 'all of God you'll ever need
for anything you'll ever face'. He says,
'My grace is sufficient for you'. When
you have him you have it all.

For Further Reflection

Revelation 1:4
2 John 3

Let God provide

One of God's names is *'Jehovah-Jireh',*
which means 'the provider of all'.
By virtue of this name God is saying,
'I'll be everything you need.'

For Further Reflection

John 16:23
1 John 3:22

Use your heavenly counsellor

Medical researchers have shown a correlation between unresolved anger and heart attacks: it seems that people who bottle up their resentment are far more susceptible than those who diffuse it by venting their emotions. You have a wonderful heavenly counsellor who will always listen to you.

For Further Reflection

Isaiah 9:6
Isaiah 59:1

Blessed hope

There is nothing like hope; it provides calm for the future. So when life hurts and dreams fade, look forward to the blessed hope of the return of our Lord and saviour Jesus Christ.

For Further Reflection

John 14:1–3